Cornerstones of Freedom

The Story of
ELLIS ISLAND

By R. Conrad Stein

Illustrated by Tom Dunnington

 CHILDRENS PRESS, CHICAGO

Library of Congress Cataloging in Publications Data

Stein, R. Conrad.
  The story of Ellis Island.

  (Cornerstones of freedom)
  SUMMARY: Describes the experiences of the many
immigrants who sought entry to the United States at
the immigration station on Ellis Island, New York,
before it closed in 1954.
    1. United States. Immigration Station, Ellis
Island, N.Y.—Juvenile literature. 2. United States—
Emigration and Immigration—Juvenile literature.
[1. United States. Immigration Station, Ellis Island,
N.Y. 2. United States—Emigration and immigration]
I. Dunnington, Tom. II. Title. III. Title: Ellis
Island.
JV6483.S83   325'.1'097472   79-12225
ISBN 0-516-04613-6

10 11 R 93 92 91

A ship steamed into New York Harbor in 1905. Hundreds of excited immigrants crowded on deck. They spoke different languages, but this morning there was only one word on their lips—America.

"There she is!" someone shouted.

The head and upstretched arm of the Statue of Liberty appeared above the morning mist. People pushed to the rail to get a better view. Mothers lifted their small children. A few people cried. Some knew the words written on the base of the great statue, "Give me your tired, your poor, Your huddled masses yearning to breathe free." All knew the Statue of Liberty welcomed them.

Almost in her shadow lay a tiny, rocky piece of land. This was Ellis Island, a giant processing center. Here an immigrant would either be allowed to enter the United States or refused and sent back to Europe. In many European languages Ellis Island was called the "Isle of Tears."

If the immigrants were lucky they passed through

Ellis Island quickly. Then they found themselves on the busy streets of a confusing city where the people spoke a foreign tongue. Most of them had just a few dollars in their pockets. Many were farm folk who would have to learn how to live in the city. Most were uneducated. All would have to take back-breaking jobs for wages of ten to fifteen dollars a week.

Still the immigrants flocked to America. Around the turn of the century more than a million people a year passed through Ellis Island. Many came from Russia, Poland, Yugoslavia, southern Germany, Italy, Sicily, and Greece. Frightened and confused, these brave immigrants left Ellis Island to enter a new life.

Why did so many millions uproot themselves from the Old World to face the hardships of life in America? That question can be answered in one word: hope. The people arriving at Ellis Island hoped, believed, and prayed they would find a better life in the United States. The overwhelming majority did.

From its beginning the United States has been a nation of immigrants. Only the American Indians can truly call themselves "native Americans."

Historians usually divide American immigration into three time periods. The colonial period ran from the early 1600s to 1776. The period of "old" immigration stretched from 1776 to 1890. The "new" immigration began when millions came to America during the 1890s and early 1900s.

Most of the immigrants during the colonial period were English and Scottish. Colonies of German and Dutch settlers also arrived. A sorry chapter in American history occurred during this period. Thousands of slaves were brought from Africa to the New World.

The period of "old" immigration was highlighted by the coming of more than two million Irish. Most of them crossed the Atlantic to escape what was called the "Great Irish Potato Famine." The famine was caused by a disease that struck Ireland in the 1840s and made potatoes rot in the fields. Since the Irish people depended almost entirely on potatoes for food, most of the country was starving. One of the Irish immigrants who came to America during the potato famine was named Patrick Kennedy. His great-grandson would become the thirty-fifth President of the United States.

After the American Civil War thousands of German, Swedish, and Norwegian farmers came to the United States. They were attracted by free land given away under the Homestead Act. Also during this time many Chinese settled on the West Coast. They worked on the railroads and in the mines.

Finally came the period of "new" immigration. Millions streamed to America to escape the hopeless poverty and over-population of southern and eastern

Europe. The mass migration of people from the Old World to the New after 1890 was like a human flood. No other country in modern history had ever experienced anything like it.

The long journey for these new immigrants began deep in Europe.

Exaggerated stories of wealth in the United States circulated freely among European peasants. America was often pictured as a Garden of Eden where poverty and hunger did not exist. "They used to tell us that the streets in the United States were paved with gold," said one woman who grew up in a Croatian village. "When I was a little girl I thought that all Americans were millionaires."

A more accurate picture of life in America came from letters from relatives who had already immigrated. "In my little village only the priest could read or write," one Italian immigrant remembered. "Whenever anyone got an 'America letter' from an uncle or a cousin the whole village would gather at the church to hear the priest read it."

Usually the "America letters" told the truth about life in the United States. The work there was hard and the money was small. Most immigrants lived in crowded apartments. Still, with enough hard work and a little luck, a person could eventually buy his own home and send his children to school. A home of one's own! An education for the children! Incredible, thought the European peasants, who had lived in poverty all their lives as had their fathers and their grandfathers before them.

Penny by penny families saved their money to pay for the trip to America. Very often the trip cost too much for the whole family, so the father went first. He would get a job and later send for the family.

Sometimes parents would save their money and send their oldest son or daughter to America. When a European left his village to immigrate he usually left it for life. Never again would he see the people and the places he once loved. One teenager told of leaving his mother and father at a train station in a small Russian town. "When the train drew into the station my mother lost control of her feelings. As she embraced me for the last time her sobs became violent and Father had to separate us. There was a despair in her way of clinging to me which I could not understand then. I understand it now. I never saw her again."

When the immigrant arrived at a European port city he soon learned a new word—steerage.

"What is this steerage?" one immigrant asked another.

"It is the basement of the ship," came the reply.

The word steerage simply means that part of a ship kept for the passengers who pay the lowest fares. Usually steerage was in the lowest deck of a steamship. One passenger in 1903 wrote, "We climbed down to steerage by going down a narrow, steep stairway. It was dark and slippery. Once there I saw people lying in bunks that were stacked up one on top of the other. The people did not have enough room to sit up in bed. The smell inside was terrible."

A steerage ticket to New York cost ten to fifteen dollars in 1910. It was the only ticket the immigrant could afford.

Most steerage passengers had never even seen the ocean before, much less sailed on a ship. A Jewish immigrant from Russia said, "A storm hit us on the second night out in the Atlantic. I remember women were screaming, babies were crying, and dishes were falling out of the top beds and breaking on the floor. We all thought the end was near." Another remembered his horrible seasickness, "I couldn't get out of bed for two whole days."

But storms did not last forever, and the Atlantic crossing was not one long ordeal. On sunny days people went up on deck. One of the immigrants might have an accordion. Others would sing. If the song was in a strange language a person could still hum the tune. One young man had never met anyone from outside his own village before, but on board ship. . . "I asked a girl to dance with me, but she did not speak Polish. I used sign language and pretty soon we were dancing all over the deck. I couldn't believe I was dancing with a girl who I couldn't speak with, not one word."

The Atlantic crossing took about three weeks. At New York Harbor the steamship first docked at Manhattan. There the first-class and cabin-class passengers got off the ship. The immigrants in steerage waited. Then a ferryboat tied alongside and the immigrants climbed aboard. Their next stop was Ellis Island.

Ellis Island is about one mile south of Manhattan. It was once used by the early Dutch settlers as a picnic ground. Immigrants used to come through a center called Castle Garden at the tip of Manhattan. But after 1885 when the stream of immigrants was becoming a flood, the federal government decided to build a new center. Ellis Island opened in 1892. Before its doors were closed more than 16 million people passed through its great hall.

As the ferryboat, jammed with immigrants, drew near Ellis Island many people began to worry. They had heard stories of immigrants who had been held there for many days. Others had been sent back to Europe. Would it happen to them? Had they saved their money for what seemed like a lifetime only to take a wasted voyage? Many of the new immigrants found Ellis Island more frightening than the ocean crossing.

One New York journalist described the first day at Ellis Island. "The day of the immigrants' arrival in New York was the nearest earthly likeness to the final day of judgment, when we have to prove our fitness to enter Heaven."

When the ferryboat docked at the island, the immigrants were herded off the boat and into one of the red brick buildings. Guards shouted, "Hurry up now. Quit poking around. We haven't got all day." The center at Ellis Island was built to handle 5,000 people daily. During the high tide of immigration more than twice that number passed through the main hall each day.

Guards tied large tags to the immigrants' coats. Each tag had a number on it. At the end of a long hallway these numbers were shouted out in Italian, Yiddish, Greek, Croatian, Polish, German, and other languages. After much pushing and shouting the newcomers were separated into groups of thirty. Then the bewildered immigrants were taken to Registry Hall. It was the largest room any of them had ever seen. A maze of aisles crisscrossed the room. Long lines of people stood in these aisles waiting to be examined by doctors or questioned by immigration officers. The noise inside was a din of shouts, curses, and crying children.

First came the doctors. Children over the age of two were made to walk to see if they had a limp. People were checked carefully by doctors. Each doctor held a piece of chalk. If a doctor suspected a heart problem, he would write a giant H on the

immigrant's coat. That immigrant would then be
sent to another room to wait for a more thorough
examination. Other letters were chalked onto coats.
F for facial rash, Sc for scalp infection, K for hernia.
The most dreaded letter of all was X. That meant
mental problems, and people marked with an X were
usually sent right back where they came from.

After the doctors the immigrant next faced the questions of an immigration officer. "What kind of work do you do? Can you read and write? How much money do you have? Have you ever been in prison?"

Immigration laws were confusing and they kept changing. For example, new immigrants were told by relatives who had already been through Ellis Island to say no when asked if they had a job waiting. "But wouldn't it sound better if I said I had a job in the United States?" the immigrant wondered. The answer was no. Having a job before entering the country broke the 1885 contract labor law passed by Congress.

About one in six immigrants was kept at Ellis Island for medical or other reasons. Those held were given hearings and further medical examinations. They could remain on the island for as long as four days. Most would finally be allowed to immigrate. But many would be sent back to Europe.

The dejection felt by those sent back was dreadful. Some, in desperation, tried to swim to Manhattan. Most of them drowned. It is difficult to imagine the suffering felt by parents who were told that three of their four children could enter America, but their fourth could not for medical reasons. Family groups were sometimes split up at Ellis Island, and children as young as ten years old were sent back to Europe alone.

An Italian-American who worked at Ellis Island as an interpreter once said, "I never managed during the years I worked there to become callous to the mental anguish, the disappointment, and the despair I witnessed daily... At best the work was an ordeal." That man would later become a famous mayor of New York City. His name was Fiorello La Guardia.

If an immigrant passed all his tests, his stay on Ellis Island lasted only about five hours. But to him the experience remained one that he would talk about for the rest of his life.

When the last question was asked and the last doctor satisfied, the immigrant was shown out of Registry Hall. He walked down a hall to a door that was labeled, curiously, PUSH TO NEW YORK. He pushed.

After a ferryboat ride the immigrant found himself in the middle of New York City. It was baffling and fearsome. Yet in many ways it was the most exciting place he had ever seen. The buildings

seemed to tower higher than mountains. One immigrant wondered why there was no snow on the top of them. Never had the newcomer from Europe seen so much traffic. Streetcars clanged down the streets. At every corner the new immigrant discovered something he had never seen before. A Polish woman wrote home, "On my first day in New York I saw both a Chinese man and a Negro woman. I knew then that I was in America." A Russian wrote, "On my first day I ate a sticky white fruit. I liked it. It was called a *panana.*"

The very first obstacle many immigrants faced was the English language. Most of them had addresses of friends or relatives, but they could not say where they wanted to go. A German hoped to go to "Linkinbra." He meant Lincoln, Nebraska. A Hungarian woman became angry when no one could understand that she wanted to go to "Szekenevo, Pillsburs." She meant Second Avenue, Pittsburgh. An eighteen-year-old Polish immigrant had borrowed an English book while on board ship. He had practiced these words over and over again, "Can you direct me to the nearest Yumka? Can you direct me to the nearest Yumka?" He wanted to go to the nearest YMCA.

Many carefully thought-out plans collapsed on that first day in New York City. One family with nine children left Ellis Island with just a few dollars. They were not worried because Uncle Otto from the old country was to meet them in New York with train tickets to Cleveland. The money for the tickets had been sent six months earlier. The family waited and waited. Uncle Otto never showed up.

A large number of immigrants stayed in New York. Soon that city had the most unusual population on earth. By 1920 New York held more Italians than Rome, more Germans than Bremen, and more Irish than Dublin. Also it was the largest Jewish city in the world.

Other immigrants scattered about the country. Most went to big cities where they could find jobs. There they gathered in neighborhoods, turning them into little Italys, little Polands, and little Germanys. They read newspapers printed in their own language. They shopped at stores that sold food from their old countries.

Neighborhoods set up by the new immigrants often resembled the boundary lines of old Europe. One man wrote about Chicago. "On a summer day when the windows were open you could close your eyes and still tell what neighborhood you were in. All you had to do was smell the cooking and figure out if it was Polish, Italian, German, or Jewish."

It took several years for the new immigrant to adjust to life in America. The first few years were the loneliest. "It is true I have work and I'm not hungry. But I have not laughed since I came to America," wrote one Greek woman. A young man from Poland wrote to a hometown friend, "I would like to marry Zoska, because girls in America are lazy and let themselves get fat. So, please, send me Zoska." A Russian wrote a long letter to his aunt telling her how much he missed his old village, but he ended his letter with these words, "But I will not go back if someone was to give me the master's estate. Once you have tasted America there is no way to go back to those old miseries."

The mass movement of people from eastern and southern Europe to the United States changed the character of the country forever. No longer were the majority of the American people from northern Europe or the British Isles. The writer Robert Bently once said of the United States, "We call England the mother country, but most of us come from Poland or Italy."

The United States was called "the Great Melting-pot" during those years when European immigrants flocked to her shores. In most cases the immigrants preferred to live with their own kind. But their children blended together easily. They went to the same school—Poles, Germans, Jews, and Italians. In Europe they might have been enemies, but in the United States they played together. The children also learned English faster than their parents and were quicker to adopt American ways.

Eventually the adults adopted American ways also. A few even changed their names to make them sound more American.

The immigrants came to the United States, worked, and obeyed the laws. But as their numbers grew, so did their enemies.

Organized labor had always been against allowing so many thousands of newcomers to enter the country. The unions said the immigrants were holding down wages. The charge was largely true. The immigrant had to take whatever job he could get, and big business knew it. Around World War I labor unions became more powerful. They pressured Congress to limit immigration.

In the East groups spoke out against immigration. They claimed the newcomers from eastern and southern Europe were "destroying the purity of the American race." One protester wrote that the new arrivals were, "beaten men from beaten races; representing the worst failures in the struggle for existence."

The Ku Klux Klan also wanted to stop immigration. They disliked the new arrivals because most of them were either Catholic or Jewish.

Because of these pressures Congress passed a new immigration law in 1921. It not only limited the number of immigrants allowed in the country, but also set up a quota system. Under the new law each country was given a quota, a fixed number of people that would be allowed to immigrate. The quota system put strict limits on countries in southern and eastern Europe.

The new law was effective. The flood of immigrants entering the country during the 1900s and 1910s slowed down to a trickle during the 1920s and 1930s. The golden gate at Ellis Island was swinging shut.

Today it is hard to understand why the immigrant was so disliked and feared by many native-born Americans. The men and women arriving at Ellis Island seventy and eighty years ago became the most productive Americans of the 20th century.

Their labor made the steel that forged modern America. Their muscle built the great cities. And their sons and daughters became the doctors, lawyers, business people, and politicians who later led the country.

The immigrants came, asking only for a chance. They brought with them a willingness to work hard and a hunger for learning. For many years the United States has been the envy of the world, thanks largely to the contributions of those amazing immigrants who once passed through Ellis Island.

Today the red brick buildings still stand on Ellis Island. The island was closed as an immigrant center in 1954. Inside the great Registry Hall today are overturned tables, broken sinks, and rusting file cabinets. Most of the windows are broken. There are now plans to turn the island into a museum dedicated to the millions who once passed through these halls hoping to find a better life.

Looking at the crumbling insides of Registry Hall, the visitor can still imagine the days of the Great Melting-pot. One can picture long lines of frightened immigrants shuffling through the aisles. Each one hoping to reach that final door that said, PUSH TO NEW YORK. When, at last, they arrived at the door, they pushed. And they built America.

ABOUT THE AUTHOR

Mr. Stein was born in Chicago of immigrant parents. His mother is from Yugoslavia and his father from Germany. Mr. Stein's mother immigrated through Ellis Island just before World War I when she was six years old. She is the Croation woman quoted in this book.

The author grew up in a Chicago neighborhood that was populated mainly by European immigrants. As a child he heard many stories from neighbors about the long Atlantic crossing and the anxiety of Ellis Island.

Mr. Stein graduated from the University of Illinois with a Bachelor's Degree in history in 1964. He later earned a Master of Fine Arts degree from the University of Guanajuato in Mexico. He is the author of many other books, articles, and short stories written for young people. Mr. Stein now lives in the town of San Miguel de Allende in Mexico.

ABOUT THE ARTIST

Tom Dunnington divides his time between book illustration and wildlife painting. He has done many books for Childrens Press, as well as working on textbooks, and is a regular contributor to "Highlights for Children." He is at present working on his "Endangered Wildlife" series, which is being reproduced as limited edition prints. Tom lives in Elmhurst, Illinois.